NIGERIAN CUISINES

A Historical Compilation of Mouthwatering Traditional Delicacies from Hausa, Yoruba and Igbo Ethnicities

Joseph Ifechukwude Chiadika

NIGERIAN CUISINES

A Historical Compilation of Mouthwatering Traditional Delicacies from Hausa, Yoruba and Igbo Ethnicities

iUniverse books may be ordered through booksellers or by contacting:

iUniverse
1663 Liberty Drive
Bloomington, IN 47403
www.iuniverse.com
1-800-Authors (1-800-288-4677)

ISBN: 978-1-5320-7506-3 (sc)
ISBN: 978-1-5320-7508-7 (hc)
ISBN: 978-1-5320-7507-0 (e)

Print information available on the last page.

iUniverse rev. date: 05/10/2019

CONTENTS

DEDICATION

To The Ever Living Water with Whom no one could ever thirst or hunger.

ACKNOWLEDGEMENTS

This cook book wouldn't have been made was I not made by the greatest maker; the pillar of life and the creator that was never created-Jehovah Elohim. To Him belong all wisdom and knowledge and my thanks are ever flowing before Him!

My mom, friend and confidant; my greatest cheerleader and my moonbeam; Kathleen Dommer deserves a zillion thanks and more for her never-dwindling love and encouragement.

To all members of my immediate family and everyone who believes in me; I say a big thank you. I wish to specially acknowledge all lovers of Nigerian foods...*Daalu nu Shinne (Thank you very Much)!*

PREFACE

What shall it profit one to gain the whole world and starve his body of good food? Emphatically, NOTHING! Good food is good health, good life and the best elixir of longevity.

Nigerians are aware of the aforementioned and that explains why we enjoy varieties of good food that keeps us closer to the kitchen. Nigerian wives are aware that the way to a man's heart is the quality of food he eats and thus, they do all they can to keep the kitchen department filled with the aroma of good food every day.

This book cannot claim to be an encyclopedia of all Nigerian foods but it sure could pass for a compendium of the most delicious and mouthwatering Nigerian soups, stew, sauce and other meals that keeps a typical Nigerian close to the kitchen.

There abounds a thousand and one Nigerian cookbooks but what stands this out is that it embraces the historical and cultural aspects of the Nigerian people. It is written in simple style and specifically written to serve both those within the Nigerian society and those in diaspora. Every ingredient contained in this cookbook can easily be accessed by all and sundry. The recipes are basically for a family size of 3-5 persons.

Finally and importantly, I acknowledge my grandmothers who taught me how to cook and writers of Nigerian cookbooks whose books were consulted while writing this. I take full responsibilities for any errors or shortcomings of this book, as such your criticisms and confrontations are welcome.

Read it! Cook It!! Love It!!!

Joseph Chiadika

AUTHOR'S CONTACT INFORMATION

For enquiries, suggestions, constructive criticisms and additional information, feel free to contact the author.

NAME: JOSEPH CHIADIKA

NATIONALITY: NIGERIAN

PHONE NO: +2348168403541

EMAIL: ifyjoe44@gmail.com

INTRODUCTION

Nigeria is a country in West Africa. Until October 1, 1960 when the Nigerian nation got her independence, it was one of the colonies of the British government.

There are over 500 ethnicities in Nigeria, each with their specific languages and culture. The diversity of Nigeria as a country is what makes it unique. Due to this ethnic and cultural diversity, the Nigerian foods come in different forms and makes. In other words, each ethnic group in Nigeria has its own type of food and recipes. It is, therefore, safe to say that there are over 500 Nigerian foods!

In this cook book, efforts shall however be made to introduce you to the best of all Nigerian foods with specific attention to Nigerian Soups, Rice, Porridge, Desserts, Appetizers and Beverages.

To better appreciate the Nigerian foods and the Nigerian people, let's have a brief detail about the major ethnicities in Nigeria and these include Hausa, Yoruba, and Igbo.

HAUSA

The Hausa is a major and the biggest ethnicity in Nigeria. With a population of about 67 million, the Hausa ethnicity makes up approximately 25% of the Nigerian population. The Hausa ethnicity is a diverse but culturally humongous people based mainly in the northern and northwestern part of the country. Its culture is homogenized and the people are found in almost all parts of the country. They are known mainly for raising cattle and other livestock, growing crops, (primarily vegetables such as tomatoes) and trading.

- The Hausa people are predominantly Muslims, that is, their major religion is the Islam. Politically, the Hausa people have always been in the forefront of the Nigerian political face majorly because of their large population and earlier romance with the British Colonial government. The Hausa people have a number of delicious meals that you cannot miss to taste. Such meals include the Tuwon Shinkafa and Miyan Taushe Soup.

YORUBA

The Yoruba ethnic group is the second largest ethnicity in Nigeria which makes up approximately 21% of the Nigerian population. The Yoruba people are mostly found in the Western and South Western parts of Nigeria and are predominantly identified as Christians and Muslims though a large number of the Yoruba people still uphold the traditional religion of their ancestors.

They are well known for their cultural traditions, including music, festivals and traditional arts and architecture. The Yoruba people have remained an intricate part of the Nigerian politics even before the Nigerian independence in 1960.

They have a number of delicious delicacies including *Amala, Ofada Rice and Efo Riro Soup.*

IGBO

The Igbo ethnic group in Nigeria makes up approximately 18% of the Nigerian population. The Igbo people are mainly settled in the Eastern/Southeastern part of the country but are found in almost every part of the country. They are mostly known for their business acumen. The Igbo have been an essential part of the oil trade in Nigeria's southeastern region.

In 1967, upon the declaration of the Republic of Biafra by Odumegwu Ojukwu, the Igbo people fought with the Nigerian government to achieve independence. The war lasted about two and a half year in which they were subjected to dire conditions with many starving to death. Since the war, the Igbo people have been reintegrated into the Nigerian society; yet they still feel marginalized by the status quo in Nigeria and the Nigerian politics.

The Igbo people enjoy a number of nutritious delicacies including the *Uha Soup and Ofe Onugbu*.

NIGERIAN
Soups and Recipes

There are a variety of Nigerian soups. The different ethnicities within the Nigerian society have different kind of soups that are peculiar to them. These are very delicious and nutritious. In this section, we shall be discussing the soups with the particular people of Nigeria that enjoys them as well as offer comprehensive recipe and direction on how to make them.

Soups are very essential in the Nigerian food recipes as they constitute over 70% of the Nigerian food. All Nigerian soups can be served with Eba (Garri), Amala and Starch (We shall discuss these later). There's no fast rules on making Nigerian soups as per the measurements, so the outcome of the soup often depends on the cook's creativity and number of persons that will eat the soup as well as the occasion for which the soup is being prepared. The recipes contained herein are for a family size of 3-5 persons.

OGBONO SOUP

Ogbono Soup is a Nigerian soup made with ground dry Ogbono Seeds (Ogbono is local name for Irvingia Seeds). The Ogbono soup has a mucilaginous (slimy) texture and can be eaten with Eba (Garri) or any choice staple food. The Main Ingredients for Ogbono soup include:

- 1/2 cup of Ground Ogbono Seeds
- 1 and 1/3 cup of palm oil
- Leaf Vegetables (Bitter leaf, pumpkin leaf or celosia)
- Ground/Dry Crayfish or Shrimp
- Fish (Stockfish)
- Meat (Beef, Pork, Chicken etc)
- Seasonings (Chili pepper or ground pepper, salt, onion and seasoning cubes like Knorr)

With the above ingredients, you are sure to have a delicious Ogbono soup. Once you have these ingredients, proceed to the kitchen and:

> Soak the stockfish with hot water for few seconds and then wash once
> Cut your meat into sizes and wash
> Parboil your meat with all the necessary ingredients (Seasoning cubes, salt, onions) until it is soft enough for consumption.
> Add more water at this point (be careful not to add too much water). Add the washed stock fish, palm oil, ground crayfish.
> Stir, cover and cook for 10-15 minutes
> Add salt (remember there's salt in the meat) and pepper to taste, add another seasoning cube, add the ground Ogbono seeds, stir and cook for another five minutes (Do not cover at this point)
> Taste your soup (you can add more salt, pepper or seasoning cube depending how the taste you get). If it's too thick, you can add more water. Add any of the leaf vegetables (preferably bitter leaf). Stir and allow simmer for three minutes after adding the leaf vegetable.
> You just made a very delicious Nigerian Ogbono soup.

EFO RIRO SOUP

E fo Riro is a popular Yoruba soup. The name 'efo' means 'vegetable'. Therefore, it is a local Yoruba vegetable soup/stew. It is very rich and nutritious. It can be served with Amala, Fufu or Eba.

Efo Riro soup takes approximately 60 minutes to prepare depending on the availability of ready ingredients and the cook's cooking pace. Below are the ingredients to prepare the soup for 5-6 persons. The cook can increase or decrease the ingredients depending on the audience or taste. The ingredients include:

- Sliced Spinach leaves
- Stockfish
- Smoked fish
- Assorted meat (1kg)= 2 1/4 lbs
- 2-3 medium sized bell pepper (sliced)
- Sliced 2-3 fresh red pepper
- Sliced 4-5 fresh tomatoes (optional)

- 1 big onions
- 2 cooking spoon of ground crayfish
- 2-3 spoons of Iru (Locust Bean or Dawadawa)
- Palm Oil (200ml)
- 3 Knorr cubes

With the above ingredients ready, the next step is to begin the preparation of Efo Riro Soup:

> Place your washed assorted meat in a pot, add a little water, season with salt, sliced onions, 2 knorr cubes and allow to boil for 10 minutes; add 1-2 cups of water and cook till it is soft and the water is almost dried.
> Add the smoked fish or any other type of fish, stockfish, a cup of water and cook for another 10 minutes till the water is almost dried.
> Remove the pot from heat, place another pot on heat and pour your 200ml of palm oil. Allow to heat for a minute, add sliced onions, bell pepper, red pepper and/or fresh tomatoes, stir and allow to fry for 10 minutes while stirring occasionally to avoid burning.
> Add the cooked meat and fish, stir and allow to simmer for 5-6 minutes; add the ground crayfish, Iru (locust bean/dawadawa), stir and allow to simmer for 2-4 minutes.
> Off your heat and serve the delicious soup you just made with either Fufu, Eba, Amala, pounded Yam or any other Nigerian food.

OWO SOUP

Owo soup is a delicious traditional Nigerian soup popular among the Urhobo, Isoko, Itsekiri (Delta State) and Benin (Edo) people of South South region of Nigeria. It is mostly prepared during traditional activities such as marriages and can be prepared for home use too. The soup is meant to be consumed immediately.

The Owo soup is made with palm oil and garri or starch as thickener among other ingredients. In a glance, the following are the *major ingredients* for Owo Soup for 2-3 persons:

- 1 and 1/3 cup of palm oil
- 1 medium sized lump of Akanwu (African Potash)
- Dried fish (cat fish or any other type of fish)
- Dried crayfish
- Shrimp
- 1 tablespoon of dry ground pepper
- $1^{1/2}$ handful of garri (to be used as thickener)
- 1 knorr cube
- Salt to taste

To cook Owo soup, the cook should:

> Wash the dried fish, crayfish and shrimp. Put them in a clean pot. Add ground pepper to your taste, add salt, knorr cube, a cup of water and palm oil. Set on heat and allow to boil for 10-15 minutes.
> While its cooking, put your garri (as thickener, be careful not to make it too thick) in a bowl, add little water so that the garri can absorb, grind the akanwu (African potash) and add to the garri bowl, take some hot water from the boiling pot, add it to the garri bowl and stir thoroughly until everything dissolves.
> Pour the content of the bowl into the pot on heat and stir continuously (reduce the heat at this point and be close by because at this stage, it will foam).
> After 5 minutes, put down the pot and your Owo soup is ready to be served with Starch, Pounded Yam or Fufu.

OHA SOUP

Oha soup, popularly called *"Ofe Oha"* is popular among the Southeastern (Igbo) part of Nigeria. It is a traditional soup cooked with the Nigerian Oha leaves. The oha leaves are seasonal and may not be found fresh all year round, therefore, you could make use of the dry oha leaves in the absence of the fresh ones.

Oha soup is similar to the Bitter leaf soup (Ofe Onugbu); the only difference is the vegetables. While Oha soup is cooked with Oha leaves, Ofe Onugbu is cooked with Bitter leaves. The following includes the ingredients for cooking Oha soup for 4-6 persons:

- Oha leaves (Fresh or Dry)
- 8 small corms or bulbs of cocoyam (elephant ear bulbs) or alternatively, use cocoyam flour
- 3 cooking spoons of red palm oil
- Beef/assorted beef include Fresh meat and Shaki (cow tripe)
- Assorted fish (Dry fish and stockfish)
- Blend Chilli pepper (depending on your taste), salt and ground crayfish
- 2 knorr cubes
- 1 teaspoon of Ogiri Igbo (locust bean/ dawadawa)

Before you start cooking:

> Blend your chilli pepper and set aside
> Put a half litre of water in a pot and set on heat. Just before it starts boiling, slowly turn in your cocoyam flour and stir simultaneously. Keep turning the flour and stirring until you feel its getting strong, then stop adding the flour and stir the flour very well until it has formed into a smooth paste and then turn the paste onto a plastic plate.
> Using your fingers, cut the fresh oha leaves into tiny pieces. This is done to prevent the oha leave from getting darker when cut with a knife. If you are using the dried oha leaf, soak in water for 5 minutes before adding it to the soup.

Now that all your ingredients are ready:

> Put the assorted beef (shaki or cow tripes), dry fish and stock fish in 1 litre of water, season with onions, salt and 1 knorr cube and boil till they are cooked. The sign of a cooked Shaki is that the cuts will start curling on itself.
> Wash the beef and add to the pot of cooked shaki etc and continue cooking.
> When the beef is cooked, add pepper, Ogiri Igbo (locust bean or dawadawa), 1 knorr cube and ground crayfish and cook for 10 minutes. Add the cocoyam flour paste in small lumps and then the palm oil.
> Cover the pot and cook on high heat till all the cocoyam lumps are dissolved. You can add more water if the soup seems too thick.
> Add the cut fresh oha leaves or soaked dried oha leaves and cook for 2 minutes.
> Stir and taste. You could add more salt or pepper if need be, allow to cook for a minute or two and the soup is ready. Serve with Eba, Semo, Fufu, Amala or pounded yam!

BITTER LEAF SOUP (OFE ONUGBU)

L ike the Oha soup, bitter leaf soup is native to the Igbo people of Nigeria. The ingredients and processes of making the soup is similar or exactly the same with that of Oha soup. The only difference is that the bitter leaf is used here.

Follow the following process to make your Nigerian Oha soup:

> Put the assorted beef (shaki or cow tripes), dry fish and stock fish in 1 litre of water, season with onions, salt and 1 knorr cube and boil till they are cooked. The sign of a cooked Shaki is that the cuts will start curling on itself.
> Wash the beef and add to the pot of cooked shaki etc and continue cooking.
> When the beef is cooked, add pepper, Ogiri Igbo (locust bean or dawadawa), 1 knorr cube and ground crayfish and cook for 10 minutes. Add the cocoyam flour paste in small lumps and then the palm oil.
> Cover the pot and cook on high heat till all the cocoyam lumps are dissolved. You can add more water if the soup seems too thick.
> Add the cut fresh Bitter Leaf leaves or soaked dried Bitter Leaf leaves and cook for 2 minutes.
> Stir and taste. You could add more salt or pepper if need be, allow to cook for a minute or two and the soup is ready. Serve with Eba, Semo, Fufu, Amala or pounded yam!

SEAFOOD PEPPER SOUP

A re you in a cold season and feeling very cold and need some hot meal? The Nigerian seafood pepper soup is an answer to your needs! It is a rich, healthy and nutritious soup mostly enjoyed during the cold seasons.

The seafood pepper soup is enjoyed by almost all ethnicities in Nigeria. There are little variations in taste when prepared by the different ethnicities in Nigeria but at the end, they're all very rich and delicious!

The following are the main and general ingredients for the Nigerian seafood pepper soup:

- 1 medium sized Tilapia/Catfish or any other lower-fat fish
- 150g or 1/3 lb of Shrimps
- 150g or 1/3 lb of sea snails (periwinkles)
- 1 tablespoonful of ground crayfish
- 2 spoonful Pepper Soup Spice Mix (See THX's African pepper soup spice mix)

- One chopped medium sized onions
- Salt (to taste)
- Blend and sliced Chili pepper
- 1 knorr cube/1 tablespoon seasoning powder
- Scent leaf

With all the ingredients ready, you should:

> Put cut and washed tilapia/catfish into a pot, add water to slightly cover the fish, add onions, pepper, knorr cube (or seasoning powder) and salt. Parboil for 5 minutes.
> Add the washed sea snails, shrimps, ground crayfish, blend and sliced chili pepper and pepper soup spice mix and cook until all the seafood are done cooking (This takes about 10 minutes more or less)
> Add sliced scent leaves and leave to simmer for 30-35 seconds and serve hot.

You could serve the Nigerian seafood pepper soup as a meal or with boiled plantain, boiled yam, rice or potatoes.

ABAK MBAKARA SOUP

The Abak Mbakara Soup is made from palmnut fruits and is native to the Niger-Delta areas of Nigeria. It is similar/the same to the banga soup. The only difference is that the Abak Mbakara soup is the seafood version of the banga soup. The following are the ingredients for Abak Mbakara soup:

- 1 can of palm nut fruit concentrate sauce (see Trofai palm nut sauce) or 2kg fresh palm fruits
- 1 big sized fresh fish (Tilapia, catfish or any other)
- 1 cup of periwinkles (or sea snail) or shrimps
- 1 fresh yellow pepper or scent pepper (chopped)
- 2 tablespoon of ground crayfish
- 1 medium sized onions (chopped)
- 2 knorr cubes or a tablespoonful of seasoning powder
- Salt
- Water leaves (Water Spinach)

With the above ingredients ready, you:

> Wash and cut the water leaves (water spinach) and set aside
> Clean and cut the fresh fish, season with onions, 1 knorr cube or seasoning powder and salt and parboil for 3 minutes. After parboiling, set the parboiled fish aside
> If you are using the fresh palm fruit, parboil till it becomes soft; then pour into a mortal and gently pound and extract the oily pulp. Add a little hot water to help scoop out the extract; and then transfer into a pot. But if you are using the canned palm nut fruit concentrate extract, simply pour the extract into the pot and leave to boil for 5-10 minutes.
> Add the sea snails (periwinkles) or shrimps and continue boiling for another 10 minutes
> Add the ground crayfish, pepper and the remaining knorr cube. Mix well and add the parboiled fresh fish and the liquid from the parboiled fish; gently stir and leave to simmer for 5 minutes
> Add the water leaves and adjust for salt or pepper. Allow it to simmer for 2 more minutes and bring the pot down
> Serve with fufu, starch or any food of your choice

EGUSI SOUP

E gusi soup is about the most popular Nigerian soup. It is enjoyed by virtually all ethnicities in Nigeria and its served in all level of Nigerian restaurants. The major ingredient in Egusi soup is ground melon seed which is rich in oils and proteins. The following are the ingredients for a typical Nigerian Egusi soup:

- Some pieces of beef
- Some pieces of cow skin
- Stock fish
- Smoked fish
- Some pieces of shaki (beef tripe)
- 2 cups of Egusi (Melon seed)
- Dried bitter leaves
- Blend fresh tomatoes and pepper

- 2 large onion bulbs(chopped)
- 1 table spoon of ground crayfish
- 4 bulbs of yellow pepper
- 1 beef seasoning cube
- 1 knorr cube
- 200ml of palm oil
- Salt to taste

Now, with all these ingredients in place:

> Season the beef, shaki and pomo (cow skin), ½ onion, 2 chopped yellow pepper and salt. Add a cup of water and steam till the water is dried
> Add more water and continue to boil till the meat is almost cooked
> Add the stock fish, smoked fish and ground crayfish and cook for 10 minutes and set the pot aside
> Set a frying pan on heat and add the palm oil. Heat the palm oil for like 30 seconds and add chopped onion, the tomatoes/pepper and fry for 10 minutes or until the Egusi is dry
> Pour the fried Egusi into the pot of meat, add a litter of water (be careful not to add too much water), add salt and seasoning cube and boil for 10 minutes
> Add the bitter leaf or any other vegetable, taste for salt and cook for 3 minutes and your soup is ready.

MIYAN TAUSHE SOUP

Miyan Taushe soup is made with pumpkin and is native to the Northern part of Nigeria. It is commonly eaten with fufu and rice. It is usually eaten during Ramadan so it is safe to call it a festive dish. Below are the ingredients for Miyan Taushe:

- 1.5 lbs of goat meat
- 1.5 lbs pumpkin peeled and cut into shapes
- ½ cup of palm oil
- ½ cup of roasted peanuts
- 7 fresh tomatoes
- 2 large onions

- 1 bell pepper
- 4 scotch bonnet peppers
- 10 oz chopped spinach
- ¼ cup of ground crayfish
- 2 tablespoon shrimp bouillon or 2 knorr cubes
- Salt to taste

After gathering the above ingredients, you:

> Slice the 2 onions and 2 scotch bonnet peppers and set aside
> Blend the peanuts and set aside
> Wash the goat meat, cut into pieces, season with the sliced onions, scotch bonnet pepper, 1 teaspoon of shrimp bouillon or 1 knorr cube and one teaspoon of salt and cook for 10-15 minutes or until the meat is soft.
> While the goat meat is being cooked, blend the tomatoes, bell pepper, 1 onion and two scotch pepper. Pour into a pot and cook on medium heat until the sauce reduces down to a thick paste
> Add the cut pumpkins and a liter of water to the cooked meat. The water should cover the meat and pumpkin. Cover and boil for 10 minutes or until the pumpkin is soft.
> Use the back of your spoon to smash the soft pumpkin, add in the blend peanuts, tomatoes paste, 1 knorr cube and stir. Cover and cook for 5 minutes on a low-medium heat
> After the cooking for 5 minutes, add the palm oil, chopped spinach, cover the pot and cook for another 5 minutes on a low heat
> Taste for seasoning and adjust salt when necessary. Turn off the heat and the soup to sit for 5 minutes and serve hot.

OKRA SOUP

Okra soup is a multi-ethnic Nigerian soup. It is enjoyed by all ethnicities in Nigeria. For instance, the Hausas (Northern Nigeria) call it Miyan Kubewa. It is in fact one of the easiest and quickest Nigerian soups to prepare. It's main ingredient is a green edible vegetable called Okra (Okro) known in many English speaking countries as "ladies' fingers or Ochro". The following are the ingredients for the preparation of this Nigerian soup:

- 250g of Okra fingers (1/2 lb)
- 3 cooking spoon of palm oil
- Beef
- Fish (Mackerel/Titus, dry fish, stockfish)
- 2 tsps of ground crayfish
- 4 bell pepper and 3 fresh tomatoes
- 1 medium sized onion bulb
- Nigerian Pumpkin leave or spinach
- 2 knorr cubes
- Salt

Before you begin cooking, you:

> Cut the okra fingers into tiny pieces. To achieve this, make a few vertical cuts followed by horizontal cuts on the okra fingers and set aside in a plate
> Blend the bell pepper and tomatoes
> Wash your vegetable (pumpkin leaves or spinach) and cut into tiny pieces
> Soak your stock fish in hot water

Once all these are ready, begin your cooking by:

> Wash and cut your beef and place it in a cooking pot. Add the soaked stockfish and dry fish. Season the beef with salt, 1 knorr cube, ½ onion (chopped) and cook till the beef and stockfish is cooked and set aside.
> Put a dry pot on heat and add palm oil and allow to heat for some seconds. Add the blend tomatoes, pepper and onion and fry for 3 minutes. Add the cut okra fingers and continue frying; add some meat stock (water from the cooked meat) from time to time till you notice the okra start to draw. This process should take a maximum of 5 minutes to avoid overcooking the okra.
> Add all the meat stock and the contents. Add the fish (mackerel or titus), ground crayfish, salt and the remaining seasoning cube and stir well.
> Add the vegetable (pumpkin leaves or spinach) and stir. Allow to simmer for 3 minutes and it is ready to be served.

NIGERIAN
Stew and Sauce Recipes

Nigerians enjoy a variety of stew and sauces. These are eaten with rice, yam and any other kind of food and no matter what combination; they usually turn out tasty and delicious. In this cookbook, we shall explore five Nigerian stew and sauce.

OFADA STEW/AYAMASE

The Ofada Stew (Igbo) or Ayamase (Yoruba) is a tasty, spicy and delicious Nigerian stew that leaves you wanting some more. The Ofada stew is so called because it is used to eat the locally produced Igbo rice called the ofada rice (abakaliki rice). However, it can be used to eat any kind of rice and yam.

Below are the ingredients for Ofada Stew/Ayamase:

- 7 Large Green bell peppers
- 4 Green scotch bonnet peppers
- Assorted meat (beaf, cow foot, cow stripe and cow skin)
- Dry fish and stockfish
- ¼ cup of ground crayfish

- 1 tablespoon of Iru (Dawadawa)
- 3 large onions
- 2 stock cubes
- Salt to taste
- 300ml of palm oil
- 300 ml of vegetable oil

When all the ingredients are set;

> Coarsely blend all the peppers and 1 large onion. Pour the blended mixture into a dry pot and heat until all the liquid are dried up and set aside

> Wash and cut the beat into sizes, season with 1 onion, 1 stock cube and salt and cook until tender. It is advised to cook the tougher meat first which could be the cow foot and tripe and add the beef and cow skin after 15minutes. Add the dried fish and stock fish and cook for 5 more minutes and set aside.

> Pour the palm oil in a pot and put on heat for some minutes and add the vegetable oil. Allow to heat for 2 minutes then add chopped onion and dried out mixture of pepper and onions. Cook for 20 minutes and add the meat stock and content, iru (dawadawa or locust beans), crayfish, 1 stock cube and salt to taste. Stir thoroughly and allow to simmer for 10 minutes and your ofada stew/ayamase is ready to be served with rice, boiled yams, potatoes or boiled plantain (unripe or ripe).

Note: If you're making for more than 6 persons, you could add a mixture of ripe (red) or unripe (green) tomatoes to increase the quantity of the stew.

TIN TOMATOES STEW

The tin tomatoes stew is a popular Nigerian stew that could be used to eat rice or boiled yam. It is prepared using tinned or canned tomatoes puree and paste. The following are the ingredients for your Nigerian tin tomatoes stew:

- 1,600g tinned tomato puree 3 1/2 lbs
- 400g tinned tomato paste 3/4 lb
- Vegetable oil (a generous quantity)
- 1.2kg of chicken 2 1/2 lbs
- 1kg of beef 2 1/4 lbs
- 2 ½ large onions

- 2 stock/seasoning cubes
- 1 tablespoon of thyme
- 1 table spoon of Nigerian curry powder
- 4 large scotch bonnet pepper
- Salt

To make the stew:

> Cut the chicken and beef into sizes, wash and place in a pot. Season with 1 onion (chopped), thyme, curry powder and salt. Cook until its tender, remove the meat from the meat stock. You could grill or deep fry the meat and set the stock aside.
> Blend the scotch bonnet pepper and ½ onion and set aside
> Place a pot on heat, add the vegetable oil. The oil should be generous enough to fry the tomato puree and paste. Allow to heat for some minutes. Now, add the remaining onion (chopped) and fry for 2 minutes and then add the 1,600g tinned tomato puree and blend scotch pepper and continue to stir for about 10 minutes.
> Add the 400g of tinned tomato paste and continue to fry until the its almost dry and looks cracked.
> Add the meat stock, 1 stock cube and salt (to taste) and the grilled or fried meat and cook for 10 minutes
> Serve with rice or boiled yam

BANGA STEW

If you are looking at making a stew for your boiled white rice and you wish not to use vegetable oil, the Nigerian banga stew is your best option. The Banga stew is made from palm fruit extract and is very nutritious.

The banga stew is very popular and indigenous to the Eastern part of Nigeria (Igbo people). The following are the ingredients for banga stew:

- Meat (chicken, beef etc)
- 800g of tinned palm fruit extract 1 3/4 lb
- 1 tablespoon of thyme
- 1 table spoon of curry
- 4 large scotch bonnet pepper
- Scent leaves
- 2 stock/seasoning cubes
- 2 onion bulbs

Once you got all the ingredients ready;

> Blend the scotch bonnet pepper and 1 bulb of onion and set aside
> Wash and cut the meat into bite sizes, season with salt, 1 stock cube, 1 onion (chopped), thyme and curry and cook until the meat is tender
> Add the tinned palm fruit extract to the pot of meat and blend scotch pepper and mix thoroughly. Cover the pot and cook for 15-20 minutes
> Add the scent leaves (cut into tiny pieces), salt (to taste) and the remaining stock cube and stir. Allow to simmer for 5 more minutes and your banga stew is ready to be served with boiled white rice.

EGG SAUCE

This is a popular and common sauce for Nigerians. It is mostly served with boiled or fried yam. Its main ingredients include:

- 6 raw eggs (chicken eggs)
- 1 red scotch bonnet pepper (sliced)
- 1 green pepper (Sliced)
- 300ml of vegetable oil

- 1 large onion bulb (Sliced)
- 1 stock/seasoning cube
- 4 fresh tomatoes (sliced)

Once you've gotten your ingredients set;

> Slice your tomatoes, scotch bonnet pepper, green pepper and onion.
> Set your frying pan on heat and add just 200ml of vegetable oil and allow it to heat for one minute before adding the sliced tomatoes, onions and peppers. Fry for 10-15 minutes. Once it is well fried, add salt and the stock/seasoning cube and stir
> Beat the eggs in a separate plate, add a pinch of salt and mix it properly. Pour on top of the frying tomato, pepper and onions; allow a minute and then stir. Break the eggs with your spoon into further tiny crumbs and serve.

VEGETABLE SAUCE

The Nigerian vegetable sauce can be served with boiled white rice or yam. It is simply delish and easy to prepare. The following are the ingredients for Nigerian vegetable sauce:

- 10 fresh tomatoes (sliced)
- 2 scotch bonnet pepper (sliced)
- 1 ½ large onion bulb
- 2 stock/seasoning cube
- 1kg of assorted meat (a combination of different parts of cow meat-liver, kidney, tripe, intestine etc)

- 3 spoons of ground crayfish
- 200ml of vegetable oil
- Salt to taste
- Sliced Vegetable (fluted pumpkin or spinach)

With the above ingredients in place;

> Parboil the assorted meat with 1 stock/seasoning cube, ½ sliced onion and salt; allow to simmer for 5 minutes and add a cup of water and cook for more 20 minutes or till the meat softens
> Set your cooking pot or frying pan on heat, add 200ml of vegetable oil and allow to heat for a minute. Add the sliced tomatoes, onions and pepper. Fry for 10-15 minutes or until its almost dried. Add the cooked meat and meat stock, 1 stock cube and 3 spoons of ground crayfish and stir. Allow to simmer on low heat for 4 minutes
> Add the vegetables, stir properly and taste for salt. Allow to simmer on low heat for 4-5 minutes and off the heat
> You just made a delicious Nigerian vegetable sauce.

NIGERIAN
Rice and Recipes

Rice is a major food in Nigeria. In fact, a typical Nigerian family eats rice consistently and in different varieties. No matter what variety they come, they turn out so great and delicious. Here, we will be discussing how to make five major varieties of Nigerian rice, namely; Jollof Rice, Banga Rice, Coconut Rice, Fried Rice and White Rice with Stew/sauce.

JOLLOF RICE

This is a popular rice variety in Nigeria. The Nigerian jollof rice is made using parboiled long grain rice and the tomatoes stew. It is very delicious and if you are having a full house and you want a Nigerian meal to serve your guests, you could try this and leave your guests asking for more.

The ingredients for Nigerian jollof rice are as follows:

- 400g long grain parboiled rice
- 2.6lbs hard chicken (hen)
- 5 plum tomatoes
- 3 Red Bell peppers (tatashe)(deseeded)
- 2 onions
- A medium piece of ginger
- 200g tomato paste
- ½ cup vegetable oil for frying the tomatoes
- 2 Knorr cubes
- 1 habanero pepper (or to taste)
- 1 tablespoon thyme
- 2 teaspoons black pepper (ground)
- Salt (to taste)
- 1 tablespoon curry powder (Nigerian curry powder)
- 5 bay leaves (add this while cooking your chicken)
- 2 teaspoons liquid smoke

Once you have all the above ingredients ready;

> Repeat the process of making the Nigerian tin tomato stew except that this time you aren't using the tomato puree but you with fresh tomatoes. However, the process is still the same. Make the stew and set aside and also grill or deep fry your chicken and set aside.
> Parboil the rice. Parboiling the rice is quite simple. Pour the long grain rice into a pot; add water enough to cover the rice. Boil for 5-10 minutes. Pour the rice into a sieve, place the sieve (with the rice) into a bowl of cold water and rinse the rice twice each with fresh cold water. Leave the rice in the sieve to drain out water
> Pour the chicken stock and the tomato stew into a sizeable pot and leave to boil.
> Add the drained parboiled rice, curry powder, salt, black pepper and liquid smoke. Stir. You could add more water so that the water level is on the same level of the rice.
> Cover the pot and leave to cook on low to medium heat.

> Check constantly until the water is dried, check to taste for salt, seasoning or to ensure the rice is fully cooked. You could add more salt, seasoning and water is otherwise. Once the rice is well cooked and soft, stir with a spatula and transfer the rice to a cool container so it will stop cooking.

> Serve with Fried Plantain, Nigerian Moi Moi, Salad or Coleslaw and grilled or deep fried chicken.

BANGA RICE

This is another type of Nigerian rice. This is made using the parboiled long grain rice and the palm fruit extract or concentrate. It is yet mouthwatering Nigerian rice.

Below are the ingredients for making the Nigerian banga rice:

- 700g of Long grain parboiled rice
- 400g tinned banga (palm fruit concentrate)
- 2 smoked fish (smoked mackerels)
- 1 big stock/seasoning cube
- 1 red onion

- 1 tablespoon ground crayfish
- 1 teaspoon ground cayenne pepper
- Habanero pepper (to your taste)
- Salt (to taste)
- Scent leaves (to your liking)

Before you begin cooking;

> Rinse and cut the red onions into small pieces.
> Debone the smoked fish and break into big pieces.
> Grind the cayenne pepper.
> Dice the habanero pepper.
> Rinse the scent leaves and set aside. You may not need to cut them.
> Repeat the process of parboiling rice given above
> Pour the tinned banga (palm fruit concentrate) into the cooking pot you wish to use to cook the banga rice and mix it with water
> Add stock cube (crushed), crayfish, onions, salt and the ground cayenne pepper. Cover and allow it to boil for 3 minutes
> When it boils, add the parboiled rice. Stir and make sure the water is at the same level as the rice. Cover the pot and cook till the water is dried
> Taste for salt and to ensure the rice is cooked and add some more salt or water if necessary.
> Cover and cook on a medium heat.
> When you can no longer see the liquid in the pot but it is not yet dry, add the scent leaves, diced habanero peppers and smoked fish on top.
> Cover and continue cooking till all the liquid dries up.
> When the water dries, stir very well and turn off the heat.
> Leave to stand for 5 minutes before serving. Serve with preferably fried plantain.

COCONUT JOLLOF RICE

Made with coconut milk and tomato stew, the Nigerian coconut rice is a delicious and nutritious Nigerian rice variety.

Below are the ingredients for the Nigerian coconut Jollof rice:

- 750g long grain parboiled rice
- 500mls Tomato Stew
- 600mls Coconut Milk
- Chicken (whole chicken or drumsticks)
- Chilli pepper (to taste)
- Salt (to taste)
- 1 medium onions
- 3 stock cubes
- 1 tablespoon thyme

With the above ingredients ready, now is time to begin making your Nigerian coconut rice:

> It's assumed that you already know how to make your stew and cook your chicken
> Now is the time to extract the coconut milk. This is quite an easy task if you follow the procedure detailed in How to Extract Coconut Milk. Set the coconut milk aside.
> Repeat the process of parboiling your rice as given above and drain
> Pour the chicken stock, coconut milk and the tomato stew into the pot. Set on heat to boil.
> Once its boiling, add the drained parboiled rice, salt and pepper to taste. If necessary, add more water to bring the water level to the same level as the rice.
> Cover the pot and leave to cook on medium heat.
> Confirm that the rice is cooked by tasting. If not, add a little more water and off the heat once the water is dried.

FRIED RICE

The Nigerian fried rice has gained popularity and prominence in Nigerian birthday and wedding parties. It is a sort of intercontinental dish made with a variety of vegetables and very delicious.

The following are the ingredients for making the Nigerian Fried Rice:

- 750g long grain parboiled rice
- Vegetable Oil
- Chicken (whole chicken or chicken drumsticks)
- 100g cow liver
- 1 tablespoon Nigerian curry powder
- ½ cup green beans
- 3 carrots
- Salt (to taste)
- 3 onions (white onions)
- 3 stock/boullion cubes
- 1 tablespoon thyme
- 2 big green peppers

Before you start cooking the fried rice;

> Wash all the vegetables and peppers. Scrape and cut the carrots into tiny cubes. Cut the green beans and green peppers into small pieces of about 0.7cm long. Chop 1 bulb of onion. Set all these aside.

> Prepare the liver and chicken. Cut the chicken into sizeable pieces, season with stock cubes, onion, salt, thyme and curry and cook until it is almost done; then add the liver and cook for 5 minutes. Remove the chicken and liver from the meat stock, grill or deep fry the chicken and cut the liver into little pieces and set aside in a plate or small bowl.

> Parboil the rice using the method detailed in parboiling rice. Rinse the parboiled rice with cold water and put in a sieve so all the water drains out.

> Pour the meat stock into a sieve to remove all traces of the seasoning items used in cooking the chicken. Pour the stock into a pot and set to boil. Once the water boils, add the parboiled rice. Also, add 1 tablespoon of Nigerian curry powder, then add salt to taste.

> Make sure the water level is slightly less than the level of the rice; at most it should be at the same level as the rice. Stir the contents; cover the pot and leave to cook on medium heat till the water is dried. Make sure not to overcook the rice so that the grains don't stick together.

> Once the water is dried up, bring down the pot and transfer the rice into a cooler container

> Place a bigger pot on heat, pour a small amount of vegetable oil into the pot. The oil should not be too much but enough to fry the vegetables.

> When the oil is hot, the chopped onions and stir for 10 seconds; then add the liver and the vegetables and stir for 1 minute and pour the rice inside. You can add salt if necessary. Stir until all the ingredients are well mixed with the rice and then transfer back to the cooler container. *Note:* If the rice is bigger than the one in this recipe, you should divide the vegetables, liver and rice into smaller parts and fry part by part to ensure they are all well mixed.

> Serve with salad

WHITE RICE AND STEW/SAUCE

This is the most commonly made rice in Nigeria. It is simply cooking the long grain rice and making tomato stew or any other form of stew or sauce to serve with it. Cooking the white rice involves the following processes:

> Parboil the rice. Parboiling the rice is quite simple. Pour the long grain rice into a pot; add water enough to cover the rice. Boil for 5-10 minutes.
> Pour the rice into a sieve, place the sieve (with the rice) into a bowl of cold water and rinse the rise twice each with fresh cod water.
> Pour the rinsed rice into the pot and add water to be slightly above the rice.
> Add salt and cook till the rice grain is soft and sticking together and your white rice is made

NIGERIAN
Porridge

The Nigerian porridge is a special Nigerian meal often cooked with vegetables, grains and yam tubers. It is also a very delicious meal. The following are some of the most popular Nigerian porridge; Beans porridge, yam porridge, plantain porridge and sweet potatoes porridge.

BEANS PORRIDGE

The Nigerian beans porridge is made with brown or black eyed beans. This is a very delicious main course dish in Nigeria and can be eaten with bread, boiled yam, custard or fried plantain. The following are the ingredients for the Nigerian beans porridge:

- 700g of brown/black eyed beans
- 2 scotch bonnet peppers
- 2 knoor cubes
- 2 fresh tomatoes
- 2 onions

- 2 tablespoon of ground crayfish
- Palm oil
- Salt (to taste)
- Fish (optional)
- Vegetable

With the above ingredients, you are not ready to cook the beans porridge;

> Pick the beans to remove any form of dirt from it
> Wash with water and place inside a pot. Add water to it and boil for 10 minutes
> Pour the boiled beans inside a sieve to drain out the water. Wash again with water and pour back into the pot. Add water slightly above the beans and place back on heat. Add one onions (chopped) to it and begin boiling.
> While it is boiling, blend the tomatoes, peppers and the remaining onions and set aside
> Check the beans to see if it's cooked and tender. If it is not, add some more water but if it is cooked and tender, pour the blend tomatoes mix, ground crayfish, stock cubes and salt (to taste) and add a little water to enable the ingredients mix into the beans. Cook for 5 minutes and add the palm oil and sliced vegetables
> After 5 minutes, and the water is dried, stir thoroughly with a spoon to make sure the palm oil and the ingredients are well mixed. Allow to simmer on a low heat for 2 minutes and your beans porridge is ready to serve. Some persons add fish or vegetable to this. You can try that!

AFRICAN YAM, PLANTAIN AND SWEET POTATOES PORRIDGE

These are other types of Nigerian porridge. I joined the three together because they involve the same process except for the main ingredients which are the African Yam, Plantain (ripe or unripe) and sweet potatoes. The ingredients are the same with the beans porridge and except for the fact that you boil and wash the beans but there is totally no need to wash the yam once it is peeled and boiled for the first time. So whether you are using African yam, plantain or sweet potatoes; you will need to peel, wash and cut into a cooking pot. Boil with onion until soft and add other ingredients and your porridge is ready to be served!

NIGERIAN
Staple Foods

Nigerian soups are served with a variety of stable foods including Amala, Eba, Usi (starch), semo, pounded yam and many others. However, in this book, we shall discuss only the first three.

AMALA

Amala is a popular Nigerian delicacy made out of yam and it is mainly popular among the Yoruba of the Western part of the country. Amala is a major meal in virtually every restaurant in Western cities like Lagos and Ibadan. It is usually eaten alongside soups such as ewedu, gbegiri, okra and more.

The following are the methods for making Amala:

> Pour quantity of water you want to use in a pot and heat to a boiling point. The quantity of water depends on the quantity of yam flour you have.
> Once the water is boiled, turn off the heat and gradually begin to add the yam flour while turning with a wooden stick
> Turn the yam flour for a while, add little water and put it back on the heat to cook on low heat for about 5 minutes so as to make it cook properly.
> You can use one of your clean fingers to feel it while still on fire to be sure it is neither too soft nor too hard. If it is too soft you can add more Yam flour, and if too hard add some hot water.
> Stir well until it is very smooth.
> Turn off the heat and put down the pot
> Wrap the Amala in nylon and put it in a cooler, so as to keep it warm or you can serve immediately.

USI (EDIBLE STARCH)

U si is made from the residue collected from cassava when processing garri (Tapioca). If one cannot access this, the processed cassava starch suffices. It is a staple food popular among the Itsekiri, Urhobo and Isoko people of Delta State, Nigeria. It is usually served with Nigerian soups such as Banga and Owo. The following are ingredients for making Usi:

- 1 cup tapioca starch (or processed cassava starch)
- 2 cups water
- 1 tablespoons palm oil

Once you have the above;

> Place the starch in a non stick frying pan. Add water to it and melt the starch within by kneading it with your hands until it disintegrates and forms part of the liquid.
> Add the palm oil to the pan. Mix thoroughly with a wooden spatula, making sure there are no hardened residues underneath. It must be able to flow freely.
> Set the pan over a medium heat. Cook and stir continuously in one direction.
> Continue stirring with the spatula; this time harder. Flip it over every two minutes until the starch is properly cooked.

EBA

Eba is a staple Nigerian food that can be served with virtually every type of Nigerian soups. The beauty of this food is that it is enjoyed by every ethnicity in Nigeria. It is made from processed cassava (garri). Making Eba is a very simple process;

- Boil 2 cups of water
- Once it is boiling very well, turn off the heat and pour the water in a thick plastic bowl enough to contain it and have extra space to allow for turning. Leave some water
- Slowly pour your garri (processed cassava) into the hot. Once the garri covers the water, pour the remaining water to cover the dry garri
- allow it to soak for like 3-5 minutes and turn generously with a wooden spatula
- Serve with any type of Nigerian soup

M oi Moi is the Nigerian name for steamed bean pudding which is made from blended mixture of brown/black eyed bean, tomatoes, peppers, onions and other special ingredients.

The following are the ingredients for Nigerian Moi Moi:

- 750g of beans (brown or black eyed beans)
- 5 tablespoons ground crayfish
- 3 big stock cubes
- 1 habanero pepper
- 2 scotch bonnet peppers (to taste)
- 2 teaspoons ground nutmeg
- 800g watery tomato puree
- 2 big onions
- 20cl vegetable oil
- 2 litres of cool or warm water
- Salt (to taste)
- Iced fish (Mackerel/Titus), boiled eggs or corned beef

Once your ingredients are ready;

> About three hours before cooking the moi moi, soak and wash the beans to remove the coat. When the entire coat has been removed, place the beans in a bowl and pour enough water to cover it. Leave to soak for three hours.
> Cut the onions into pieces and set aside. Wash the habanero/scotch bonnet peppers and set aside.
> If you are using eggs, boil the eggs, peel off the shells and set aside. If you are using iced fish, cut and wash the fish, season with salt, small amount of onion (chopped) and stock cube. When the fish is cooked, separate the fish from the stock, and break the fish into smaller pieces. Sieve the stock water to remove the pieces of onions and set aside.
> Now that the beans is well soaked and tender, blend the beans, onions, crayfish and habanero/scotch bonnet peppers together with some of the water and pour the mix into a big bowl.
> Add the vegetable oil into the blended beans, add the fish or smashed corn beef (if that's what you are using), add ground nutmeg, ground crayfish and stock cubes, slowly add the stock water and stir the mixture at the same time till you get a good mix of all the ingredients. If the stock water is not enough, you can add the hot water. Make sure not to make it too watery. Add salt to taste and stir very well.

> Pad the base of a big pot with foil paper, pour some water and set on the stove. The depth of the water should be at most 1 inch.

> Get small plastic bowls or aluminum bowls that has cover. Grease with vegetable oil and dish the moi moi mix into the bowls. Add eggs to it (if that's what you are using), cover the bowls and set them into the pot. Ensure the plastic bowls are well covered with water and far from the sides of the pot.

> Place the pot on heat and cook till the moi moi is well cooked. This takes approximately 60 minutes. You could be checking the pot from time to time to know if the moi moi is cooked. Confirm that it is well cooked by putting a knife through it, if the knife is stained with Moi Moi paste, then the Moi Moi is not cooked, but if the knife just has a slight smear of Moi Moi, then it's done. Also, when you cut through the Moi Moi, the insides will be set and not watery.

> Once it is well cooked, off the heat and allow to cool off. You can serve moi moi as a main course with custard for breakfast or as a side dish to Jollof Rice, or Fried Rice.

ABOUT THE AUTHOR

Joseph Chiadika is a Nigerian of Igbo ethnicity. He is a graduate of Mass Communication and has several academic and non-academic books to his credit. This book is his first attempt into the cookbook publishing but not his first entrance to the kitchen department. He learnt to cook from his maternal and paternal grandmothers who were good chefs in their own right. He has attended several seminars and conferences on healthy living and making Nigerian foods.